The

Ingredient   Cookbook

All The Recipes Have Only 2 Ingredients!

Marjorie Kramer

Disclaimer

Books by Marjorie Kramer

1. The No-Cook, Skinny, Delicious, Nutritious Overnight Oats in a Jar Cookbook
2. The No-Cook, Skinny, Delicious, Nutritious, Oat Smoothies Cookbook
3. The 4 Ingredients Paleo Cookbook – All The Recipes Have 4 Ingredients or Fewer!
4. The 2 Ingredient Cookbook – All The Recipes Have Only 2 Ingredients!
5. The 2 Ingredient Dessert Cookbook – All the recipes have only 2 ingredients!
6. The 26 Worst Facebook Grammar Mistakes Ever & How to Avoid Them
7. Charting New Territory in ESL – What You Wish Your ESL Book Included

Introduction

I'll let you in on a secret. I hate to cook. No really, I do. I can't stand all the preparation and mess, and then have it be over in 15 minutes. For years, I so wanted something that would help me get out of the kitchen faster, so that I could enjoy my family, read, watch the news, anything! I was THRILLED when I discovered that there were actually real dishes you could make from only TWO ingredients! My dream come true! I use these whenever I can to make my job as chief cook and bottle washer be a little easier, and to give me a little extra free time more quickly.

All of the recipes have only two ingredients, with the following caveat: Salt, pepper, and butter or oil don't count. They're really used in only a few recipes, but in my book, they don't count as ingredients.

Unless you're Julia Child or Rachel Ray, and you actually love staying in the kitchen and cooking, you're going to love this book of tricks and genius.

Table of Contents

Disclaimer   **2**

Introduction   **4**

Breakfast   **7**

Baked Avocado and Egg...................7

Bird in the nest.................9

Maple Soufflé 10

Breakfast cookies.................11

Ice Cream Bread 13

Lunch and Dinners   **14**

Egg Drop Soup.................14

Salmon Spread 15

Brownie Muffins.................16

Dinners   **17**

Steak Marinade.................17

Ham Marinade.................18

Onion Pot Roast.................19

Italian Chicken.................20

Salt-Baked Potatoes 21

Luscious Potatoes.................22

Sun-Dried Tomato Cauliflower.................23

Pesto Peas.................24

Broccoli with Creamy, Roasted Eggplant Hummus.................25

Crockpot Caramelized Onions 26

Ranch Biscuits 27

Corn Waffles 28

Parmesan Bread Sticks....................................29

Snacks   **30**

Bacon- Wrapped Dates.....................................30

Cheese Crisps...31

No-Bake Date Energy Bars...............................32

Review   **33**

Breakfast

Baked Avocado and Egg

So easy, and so good! The basic recipe is 2 ingredients, avocado and eggs. Possible additions are at the bottom of this very simple recipe!

Ingredients
>   1 ripe avocado
>   2 small eggs

Directions
>   Preheat your oven to 425°F (218°C).
>   Slice the avocado in half, and remove the pit. If the resulting hole looks too small to contain an egg, take a bit out to enlarge the hole.
>   Put each avocado half in a small baking dish or on a baking sheet. Make sure that the avocado is touching either one side of the dish, or the other avocado half. This keeps your breakfast steadier.
>   Crack one egg into each avocado half. Try to get the yolk in first, so that if any egg spills out of the avocado, it will be the whites.
>   Bake in your preheated oven about 15 – 20 minutes (depending on the size of the avocado and egg), or until the egg is cooked through.
>   Remove, add any extras you want, and enjoy!

Possible additions

    crumbled cooked bacon

    sausage

    grated cheese

    tomato

    salsa

    cayenne pepper

    chopped fresh chives or other fresh herbs

    hot sauce

Bird in the nest

My Mom used to make these for us kids on Saturday mornings as a treat. Our first cooking lesson! These are quick and easy!

Ingredients (per person)
> 1 piece of bread
> 1 egg

Directions
> Crack the egg into a bowl. Make sure there are no bits of shell in it.
> Using a cookie cutter, cut a 2.5" or 3" hole out of the bread slice.
> Melt 1 tbsp butter in a pan on medium heat.
> Place the bread slice and the cut-out into the pan, and fry until golden.
> Turn them over, and reduce the heat to low.
> Pour the egg into the hole. Cover the pan and cook until the egg has set, about 3 minutes.
> Carefully flip your "bird in the nest" over, and cook for another couple minutes.
> Salt and pepper to taste.
> Serve and enjoy!

Maple Soufflé

This is a perfect breakfast recipe for a Saturday morning. Impress your significant other, or just pamper yourself with this yummy breakfast treat. Also a fantastic dessert!

Ingredients (for four)
  2 eggs
  1/3 cup maple syrup (Grade A Dark Amber is a good choice.)

Directions
  Preheat your oven to 400°F (204°C).
  Separate the eggs.
  In a small bowl, add the syrup to the egg yolks and whisk.
  In a stainless steel bowl, beat the egg whites until peaks form.
  Carefully fold the syrup and yolk mixture into the egg whites.
  Pour into four small bowls or ramekins, and place them on a baking sheet.
  Place the baking sheet in the 440°F (226°C) oven, and then immediately turn it down to 375°F (190°C). Bake until the soufflés are puffed, about 10 minutes.
  Enjoy!

Breakfast cookies

You can make these beforehand and grab two out of the fridge on your way to work, but they're simple enough so that you can make them quickly before work or school!

Ingredients

2 large, old bananas. Since bananas are different sizes, you may need to add more or less oats. You can also use fresh bananas. You can keep old bananas on hand by letting a bunch get old, and putting the whole bunch in the freezer!

1 cup of coarsely-ground oats. You can use quick regular oats or quick oats. If you use regular, give them a few chops or put them in the food processor first.

Directions

Preheat your oven to 350°F (176°C).

Mash the bananas.

Mix in the oats. If the mixture is too runny, add more oats. If you add too many oats or some of the additions, the cookies may not hold together well.

Put heaping tablespoons of the mixture on a greased or parchment-lined cookie sheet.

Cook for 15 minutes or until light brown on the bottom.

Cool completely on a wire rack.

Possible additions
chocolate chips
walnut pieces
cinnamon
raisins

Ice Cream Bread

Can you imagine? This bread will have a bit of the sweetness and flavor of the ice cream, so use your favorites! And it's so quick! Three minutes from taking out your ice cream to putting your dough in the oven.

Ingredients (for one 8" x 4" loaf pan)
>1 pint of softened ice cream (full-fat is best)
>1 ½ cups self-rising flour   (If you don't have self-rising, use 2 cups flour, 1 ½ tsp baking powder, and ½ tsp salt, sifted together.)

Directions
>Preheat your oven to 350°F (176°C).
>Grease and flour the 8" x 4" loaf pan.
>Mix the softened ice cream and flour together in a bowl.
>Pour into the loaf pan.
>Bake for 45 minutes or until a toothpick comes out clean (or with just a few crumbs.)
>Let the bread cool for a couple minutes in the pan, then transfer to a wire rack for complete cooling.
>Serve hot or cold, maybe with another scoop of ice cream! Perfect!

Lunch and Dinners

Egg Drop Soup

This is SO quick, and as tasty as you can get at a Chinese restaurant! Also way cheaper!

Ingredients
>   1 32-oz box or can of salted chicken stock
>   3 large eggs

Directions
>   In a medium pot, bring the stock to a simmer.
>   Crack the eggs into a bowl, and beat.
>   Slowly dribble the eggs into the simmering stock, stirring constantly.
>   After a couple seconds, it's done! Serve hot! Delicious!

Salmon Spread

This is a wonderful dish for a party. It serves 12, and is absolutely delicious!

Ingredients
>   12 oz of cooked and cooled salmon
>   7 ½ oz Boursin cheese

Directions
>   Flake salmon apart with a fork.
>   If the cheese isn't soft enough to mix, you can put in the microwave for 10 seconds.
>   With a mixer, combine the salmon and cheese completely.
>   Serve it cold with crackers or toast points.
>   Your guests will love you!

Brownie Muffins

This is so easy! Just mix and bake, and oh my....

Ingredients

    1 box Devil's Food cake mix
    1 15-oz can of solid-pack pumpkin

Directions

    Preheat oven to 400°F (204°C)
    Mix the pumpkin and cake mix together. That's all. Don't add anything else.
    The mixture will likely be thick.
    Either spray a muffin tin, or put paper liners into it.
    Place batter into muffin tin.
    Bake for 20 minutes.
    Makes 12 regular or 36 mini muffins.
    Now, how easy was that?

Dinners

Steak Marinade

Amazing flavor.

Ingredients
    1 part Balsamic Vinegar
    1 part Whiskey

Directions
    Combine.
    Marinate your steak for 15 minutes or more
    before you cook it. Wow!

Ham Marinade

If you're not in the mood for beef tonight, try this easy marinade on a ham.

Ingredients
>2 cups ginger ale
>1 cup mustard

Directions
>Mix together.
>You can get your ham ready by making ½ inch, diamond-shaped cuts across the top of the ham. The cuts let your marinade soak in. Pour the marinade over the ham. Bake the ham according to package instructions. While it cooks, you can re-baste the ham with the juices in the pan.
>The slower you can cook the ham, the better it will be. It gives the ham more time to bathe in the marinade, and it makes the ham more tender.

Onion Pot Roast

Just a piece of beef and some onion soup mix make magic!

Ingredients

> 1 3-lb round steak, or beef chuck roast
> 1 envelope dry onion soup mix

Directions

> Place the meat on a sheet of heavy-duty aluminum foil.
> Sprinkle the onion soup mix on the meat.
> Wrap the meat up tightly.
> Place in a roasting pan.
> Cook at 300°F (149°C) for three hours.
> You can modify this recipe by adding either a cup of burgundy wine, or a can of condensed Cream of Mushroom soup over the roast before cooking.

Italian Chicken

And if you're in the mood for chicken, here's another effortless recipe!

Ingredients
>   6 skinless, boneless chicken breast halves
>   1 16-oz bottle Italian salad dressing

Directions
>   Place the chicken breasts into a plastic container in which they fit snugly.
>   Pour the salad dressing to cover the chicken. (You can also do this in a zip bag.)
>   Put your container into the refrigerator from an hour to overnight.
>   Preheat oven to 350°F (176°C).
>   Take the chicken out of the plastic, and place in a greased 9 x 13" baking dish, without the marinade.
>   Bake for one hour, or until chicken is thoroughly cooked, and the juices run clear. (Turn the chicken during baking.)

Salt-Baked Potatoes

Surprisingly and delightfully, these potatoes do NOT taste salty.

Ingredients (per person)
> 1 Baking potato
> Bacon fat or cooking oil
> Kosher salt

Directions
> Wash the potatoes, then dry completely.
> Prick with a fork.
> Rub with oil or fat.
> Put about an inch of salt into your crock pot.
> Lay the potato on the salt.
> Cover with salt. (You can reuse the salt several times if you store it in a air-tight container.)
> Put the cover on your cooker, and cook about 2 hours on high.
> Turn off the cooker. Let the potatoes stay warm in the cooker until you're ready to serve them.
> The salt on top will be crusty. Take the potato out.
> Brush salt off. Serve!

Luscious Potatoes

These really are luscious! Wonderfully easy recipe, perfect for entertaining.

Ingredients

1 30-ounce pkg frozen hash brown potatoes, thawed
2 cups heavy whipping cream
1 teaspoon salt
1/8 teaspoon pepper

Direction

Preheat oven to 350°F (176°C).
Drain the thawed potatoes, and dry them with paper towels.
Spray a 13" x 9" glass baking dish.
Place the potatoes in the dish, and salt and pepper to taste. Toss the potatoes to coat them.
Arrange them evenly.
Pour the whipping cream over them.
Bake, uncovered, for 50-60 minutes, or until the potatoes are light golden brown.
To make it a three-ingredient recipe, layer your favorite shredded cheese over the potatoes.

Sun-Dried Tomato Cauliflower

Talk about flavor!

Ingredients
　　　　1 cauliflower head, separated into florets
　　　　1 container of sun-dried tomato pesto

Directions
　　　　Preheat oven to 450°F (232°C).
　　　　Gently stir together the cauliflower and the pesto.
　　　　Place on a baking sheet and roast for 15 minutes until crisp.
　　　　Serve!

Pesto Peas

You can also make this with any of your favorite vegetables!

Ingredients
>1 10-oz package frozen baby peas
>1/3 cup of basil pesto
>Salt and pepper to taste

Directions
>Follow the instructions on the pea package, and cook the peas.
>Drain.
>Stir in pesto.
>(Salt and pepper to taste.)
>Serve immediately.

Broccoli with Creamy, Roasted Eggplant Hummus

Oh, yes!

Ingredients (makes 4 cups)
  3 ½ cups broccoli florets
  ½ cup of creamy eggplant hummus

Directions
  Cook your florets by steaming, boiling, roasting, or grilling.
  In a bowl, pour the hummus over the broccoli, tossing it to get it the hummus all over the broccoli.
  You can serve this either hot or cold. Delicious both ways!
  If you like, you can add lemon juice and black pepper to it when you serve.
  You can also substitute any of kind of hummus, including garlic, olive, tomato, parsley, lemon, or whatever else strikes your fancy.

Crockpot Caramelized Onions

I think these are just the best idea. They go with so much! Once you cook these, you can just keep them in the fridge and use them as needed. They will be a dark golden brown, and will have a delicious, caramelized flavor. Serve them with vegetable dishes, as additions to stews, casseroles, and soups, on sandwiches, as omelet fillings, as an appetizer with ricotta or cream cheese, in spaghetti sauce, and with any grilled meat.

Ingredients

5 or 6 large yellow or white onions
¼ to ½ cup butter (You can substitute olive oil here, but not margarine.)

Directions

Peel onions. Cut off the ends.
Put the whole onions and the butter in your slow cooker.
Cover. Cook on low for about 9 - 10 hours. Adjust temp if your cooker runs hotter.
When cooked and cooled, put the onions in glass jar with a screw-on top, or in a plastic container with a sealed top.
Absolutely fantastic. You'll be eating them on everything.

Ranch Biscuits

So uncomplicated and so good!

Ingredients

> 2 ¼ cups biscuit mix
> 2/3 cup Ranch dressing

Directions

> Preheat your oven to 450°F (232°C).
> Combine biscuit mix and Ranch dressing in a bowl using a fork.
> Put parchment paper on a baking sheet.
> Shape dough into a square, about 1 ¼" high.
> Cut into 9 squares.
> Bake for 10 minutes, or until golden brown.
> Slather with butter, and oh, buddy!

Corn Waffles

These are savory, not sweet waffles, to serve beside any meal. They can also be the
foundation for a scrumptious vegetarian meal. You can serve these with some black beans and salsa for more protein and fiber. They also freeze well!

Ingredients (for 6 waffles)
>   1 6-oz pkg corn muffin mix
>   ½ cup frozen corn

Directions
>   As you prepare the muffin mix as to package instructions, just stir the corn into the batter. Also, to make the batter the right consistency for waffles, add another tablespoon or two of milk.
>   Pour some batter in a preheated waffle iron, then quickly close the lid. Don't open the iron while it's still steaming. Repeat this until all your waffle mix has been cooked.
>   Serve immediately, or freeze. When you're ready to eat them, just pop one in your toaster!

Parmesan Bread Sticks

Ingredients
1 pkg frozen puff pastry
½ cup grated parmesan cheese

Directions
Defrost the pastry until it's firm, but not soft
Preheat oven to 400°F (204°C).
Lay the dough out. Sprinkle with half the cheese.
Cut into 1/2-inch wide strips.
Twist the strips.
Place them on a baking sheet lined with parchment. Sprinkle a bit more cheese over them.
Bake for about 10 minutes. The breadsticks should be golden brown and fantastic!

Snacks

Bacon- Wrapped Dates

Two of my favorite foods together!

Ingredients
12 slices of bacon
24 pitted Medjool dates

Directions
Preheat your oven 350°F (176°C)
Cut the bacon in half.
Wrap a half piece of bacon around each date.
Put each on a parchment paper-lined cookie sheet
Bake for 20 minutes.
Broil for 5 minutes.
Cool for just a few minutes, stick a toothpick in each, and serve!
Cut your bacon in half, so that you have two pieces of half the original length.

Optional
If you like, you can also slit the dates, and stuff them with your favorite filling. Goat cheese or mango chutney are a couple good ones.

Cheese Crisps

Full of flavor!

Ingredients
 1 cup shredded Colby Jack or Cheddar
 cheese.
 2 cups Cheese Nips

Directions
 Preheat oven to 400°F (204°C).
 Coarsely crush Cheese Nips.
 In a bowl, combine the Cheese Nips with the
 shredded cheese.
 On a baking sheet lined with parchment, place
 a heaping tablespoonful every two inches.
 Bake for about 12 minutes, or until they are
 golden brown. This means they'll be crispy. If
 you take them out before this point, they will be
 chewier.
 Cool for about 2 minutes on the pan.
 Carefully transfer with a spatula to a wire rack
 for complete cooling.

No-Bake Date Energy Bars

I don't know about you, but I LOVE dates. There just don't seem to be enough recipes out there for them. These are wonderful!

Ingredients
> 1 cup of Medjool dates, soaked overnight in water. Keep the water.
> Stone ground oats

Directions
> In a food processor, pulse the water and dates until it's a thick paste. If it's not smooth and the consistency of thick jam, add a little more water.
> Add a couple of handfuls of the oats.
> Pulse until well blended.
> Slowly add in more oats until they hold together well
> Press the mixture into the square glass baking dish, about ½" thick.
> Sprinkle with more oats, if you like
> Chill.
> Cut into squares, and serve.

Review

I hope you've enjoyed reading this cookbook. These 2-ingredient dishes are so much fun, and so quick and easy, the chore of cooking really ceases to be a chore!

Be sure to pick up my other 2-ingredient book, "The 2 Ingredient Dessert Cookbook." Yes! They're desserts made from only 2 ingredients!

Enjoy this book?
Please leave a review below and let us know what you liked about this.

Books by Marjorie Kramer

8. The No-Cook, Skinny, Delicious, Nutritious Overnight Oats in a Jar Cookbook
9. The No-Cook, Skinny, Delicious, Nutritious, Oat Smoothies Cookbook
10. The 4 Ingredients Paleo Cookbook – All The Recipes Have 4 Ingredients or Fewer!

11. The 2 Ingredient Cookbook – All The Recipes Have Only 2 Ingredients!
12. The 2 Ingredient Dessert Cookbook – All the recipes have only 2 ingredients!
13. The 26 Worst Facebook Grammar Mistakes Ever & How to Avoid Them
14. Charting New Territory in ESL – What You Wish Your ESL Book Included

Printed in Great Britain
by Amazon